Why Prayers Aren't Answered

Understanding Kingdom Principles

Patricia Marlett

Copyright © 2016 by Patricia Marlett

All rights reserved.

No part of this book may be used or reproduced in any manner without written permission of the author, except for brief quotations used in reviews and critiques.

Scriptures from the King James Bible

Printed in the United States of America

Published by High Tower Publications

First Edition - 2016

ISBN 978-0-9854059-6-0

The God of my rock; in him will I trust: he is my shield, and the horn of my salvation, my High Tower, and my refuge, my savior; thou savest me from violence. 2 Samuel 22:3

Acknowledgment

I will always and forevermore acknowledge and give thanks to God. I honor, praise, and give the glory to my heavenly Father for it is by His grace that I am blessed. With the gift He has bestowed upon me, I write in His honor to glorify His name.

Also, deep appreciation to my husband, Mark, for the unwavering love and support he gives as I pursue my passion. You are my rock, I love you.

Dedication

This book is dedicated to all

who seek answers.

Table of Contents

Part I ~ The Kingdom……………………....17

Part II ~ The Gift……………………….……27

Part III ~ The Trinity……………………....39

Part IV ~ Summary……………………….…54

Part V ~ Scriptures…………………………..57

Note from the Author

If any man speak, let him speak as the oracles of God; if any man minister, let him do it as of the ability which God giveth: that God in all things may be glorified through Jesus Christ, to whom be praise and dominion for ever and ever. Amen. 1 Peter 4:11

It is with honor and glory to our heavenly Father that I take great pleasure in presenting this book to share the truth of God's Word as taught in the Scriptures, and to assure each person who reads the content on the following pages that everything God created and provided is for you. It has always been about you when God established the foundation of all His creation as we read in the Bible and continues throughout eternity. I hope you gain insight of how much you are truly loved, and how desirous the Father is for you to be with Him today and forever.

God made all things possible through His Son, Jesus, when He gave man a new and better covenant. As a beneficiary of this testament, one of the many gifts is the free will to personally decide if we want a life with Him, one that is eternal. Though it is by our choice, God wants all His children to come home to the Kingdom of Heaven. We can be with our Father this very moment, spiritually, if we become one in spirit with Christ. The first step is a desire to have a relationship with God and become a born-again child of the Father. In Christ, we are changed from a sinner to a saint and secured as a joint-heir through Jesus in the Kingdom.

I pray you are inspired to seek God and accept His Word as the guidepost for your life and maintain a relationship with your heavenly Father. Not simply know of Him, but fall in love with Him, learn His nature and understand what He has done for you and what He expects of you, His child. As a child to the parent, we should want our Father's love and a close bond with Him more than anything, ever. Only God can heal a broken body whether it is physical or emotional, only God can supply for personal and professional prosperity, and only God can give us eternal life. There is absolutely nothing permanent on this planet as this earthen place will one day be made anew to receive the New Jerusalem which will be the eternal home of every believer.

God's love, mercy, and grace are forever present and will always protect and provide for His children. We are His most precious creation, made in His likeness, for His pleasure, never forgotten or forsaken. Promises, blessings, gifts, and power are within His Kingdom, and we are personally responsible to acquire the knowledge that God has set forth in His Word, so that we may partake of these Kingdom treasures. It is important to understand the role of Christ and His purpose in fulfilling the Father's plan and to accept the

Holy Spirit as our tutor who teaches all things of God and is our advocate in the Kingdom. This is crucial to living in the spirit and receiving all that He has prepared for us.

There may, periodically, appear a redundancy as the trinities are both separate and one; God is the Father, He is the Son, and He is the Holy Ghost. A conscious effort has been made to keep the repetitiveness to a minimum. With forethought, many Scriptures are appropriately placed to serve as a reference to what God's Word says as the focus is on His truth.

Our relationship with our heavenly Father is defined in our belief, trust, and unwavering faith. We are not lost souls wandering aimlessly and helpless throughout this life, but saints made righteous and holy in Christ for the Father.

Preface

More than any other question in the forefront of a Christian's thoughts is why does God not always answer our prayers. Today, the lack of knowledge continues to envelop the believer in confusion, leaving them without understanding of God's Word. The sole purpose of this book is to provide scriptural wisdom to enlighten the individuals who seek answers.

When we understand how God set forth His Kingdom of Heaven, His trinities of Himself as the Father, the Son, and the Holy Ghost; of man with a body, soul, and spirit; and the functionality of the Kingdom through mercy, grace, and faith, it becomes very clear of our relationship with God, with Christ, and with the Holy Spirit.

There is a mathematical equation as well as a timeline to God's creation. For His children to receive the treasures within the Kingdom, the promises of blessings, and the gifts given in Christ and the Holy Spirit, we must be knowledgable of His supernatural, spiritual Kingdom. This is an absolute requirement when we are born-again into the spirit realm in Christ. We can no longer follow our carnal nature and expect spiritual resolutions.

Answered prayers for our earthen circumstances and the desire for our prosperity and good health is all given by the Father to His children; however, we must learn how to approach our heavenly Father to receive all that He has set forth for us. We each must have a personal relationship and continuous communion with Him and this is only possible in the spirit.

It is my hope that within the pages of this book, you will gain wisdom of the necessity for a strong commitment in your relationship with God, Christ, and the Holy Spirit so that you may receive answers to your prayers, always.

Part I ~ The Kingdom

The most sought after answer for the number one question asked among Christians today is why are prayers not always answered? Why is it when we pray and sometimes even gather prayer warriors to assist, there remains no answer from God? There is nothing wrong in many people praying for the same cause; however, one fervent prayer availeth much. *The effectual fervant prayer of a righteous man availeth much.* James 5:16 The answer is not in the masses, but the methodology of our prayer. So why isn't even the one fervent prayer rendering a response from our heavenly Father? The answer is in how we pray. Are we praying the way God instructed us to approach Him in His Kingdom? If we are praying with our carnal efforts and not with our spirit through the Holy Spirit, then unfortunately, our prayers are not reaching God.

Of course, He knows of our pleas before we speak them; however, if we are amiss in understanding His instructions on how to enter into His Kingdom and approach Him on His throne, then we rightfully should not expect an answer. Thus, in that time of desperation when you've waited for God's intervention and eventually succumb to ask, "Where is

God?", it would be appropriate to look inward for self evaluation. God is the Alpha and the Omega, the beginning and the end; the same yesterday, today, and tomorrow. God is where He always is, on His throne waiting for you.

For example, you are not going to obtain a private meeting with the judge in a case you are pleading in court. You will need a spokesperson to speak on your behalf and typically this is an attorney, someone acceptable to the structured environment, the courtroom, who understands the rules and regulations that govern how you may present your case. The same holds true in the Kingdom. You may only enter into the spiritual Kingdom of Heaven through a spirit mediator who stands before God and lets your request be known. Just as a judge knows the details of the case before it is presented in his courtroom, so does our King know of the reasons you come before Him in prayer.

Therefore, your prayers must be submitted through the means that God established. Our carnal attempt and on the authority of Christ's name does not release a response. Here is where it is imperative to understand the Trinity of God and the reason and role each personage has in your life. If you do not have clarity on how God set forth His Kingdom to enter within, then you are without answers to prayers. There is a purpose for Christ and a purpose for the Holy Spirit; both being God. It is mandatory to know what each provides for man.

When we seek God in prayer and there is no response, we automatically take the mindset that God decided He isn't going to help us. For reasons we cannot fathom, He chooses to not respond to our plea and provide a resolution. This is far from the truth. The reality is that we do not have the truth, though we may think we do. When we have cried out to our heavenly Father and it appears He isn't listening, we lapse into a soulful moment allowing our emotions to rule our head and heart and do what is instinctive to our nature, we blame God. Because we don't understand, we gravitate to needing a reason for our failed communications with Him, and we put the responsibility on our heavenly Father rather than ourselves. After all, there are only two parties involved: you and God. We make all kinds of excuses why it is His fault, but rarely do we consider that perhaps the error for not hearing from God is within ourselves. There is no error or mistake in perfection which is God; however, man cannot claim perfection. Therefore, it is not difficult to see where the problem lies. We should know better than to accuse the Almighty King of withholding His greatness, yet we do it anyway. Perhaps, it soothes our hurt feelings and lessens our burden for not understanding.

Instead of pointing a finger at God, we should take a deeper look within ourselves for what we may be missing in knowledge of God's Word that is preventing our receiving. Even when we believe we have done everything right, prayed the right way, believed on His Word, held our faith, and trusted He would come through but when He doesn't, we don't know why. We turn away from Him instead of searching in His Word to find what we missed. It becomes a huge mistake to blame God which only removes you from His presence, but rather you should draw closer with a heartfelt desire for His truth. God does not pull away from His children. *The Lord is good, a strong hold in the day of trouble; and he knoweth them that trust in him.* Nahum 1:7 We fall away with our lack of understanding. God is steadfast, for you are never forgotten or forsaken, His position never changes. God is love, and you are forever deeply loved. *He that loveth not, knoweth not God, for God is love.* 1 John 4:8 With an all encompassing agape love for you, it is impossible for God to withhold His greatness in your life.

God set forth everything man would require in his earthen lifetime at the foundation of His creation. There is nothing that will ever need to be added, changed, altered, corrected, or withheld for any reason. Knowing that God has prepared for our lives, planned our destiny, knows every hair on our head, and knows what we will come to Him in prayer before we utter the first word, then surely we are the ones amiss. This is where we must learn His Word and know exactly how to enter into the Kingdom of Heaven to approach the throne of our Almighty King. *Receive my instructions, and not silver; and knowledge rather than choice gold.* Proverbs 8:10

If we haven't studied His instruction manual (Bible) and read carefully the chapter on "How to receive answered prayers," figuratively speaking, then the fault for failing the *test* is ours not the instructor. *Apply thine heart unto instruction, and thine ears to the words of knowledge.* Proverbs 23:12 God is telling us what we must do, educate ourselves in spiritual wisdom through the tutor He gives to us, the Holy Spirit, that we may learn how to live within the spirit realm, His Kingdom, and receive supernatural power.

God reveals Himself to man as the Father, the Son, and the Holy Ghost. God presented Himself to the Israelites as Himself at Mount Sinai when He came down in the cloud and spoke to them after removing them from bondage in Egypt. In the era that God was dealing with the Israelites, He communicated with them through His appointed people, or prophets. They did not have Christ and the Holy Spirit. It is in these past two thousand years since Christ, that we are privileged to have Christ and the Holy Spirit, for a personal relationship with God. *This is the covenant that I will make with them after those days, saith the Lord, I will put my laws into their hearts, and in their minds will I write them; and their sins and iniquities I will remember no more.* Hebrews 10:16-17 Within every child born into the Kingdom of Heaven, God lives in your heart as the Holy Spirit for a personal relationship with you.

One of the Kingdom precepts (laws) is that we must *ask* for anything we need of God (note: this is not referring to materialistic possessions, but receiving Spirit gifts from the Spirit Kingdom). God does not arbitrarily throw gifts down from Heaven to His children. As we are required to ask to be born into the spirit realm (free will), this should be our first clue that we also must ask for His promises of blessings, gifts, and supernatural power that has been established for us....*for the asking*. As a child, surely you remember your parents teaching you to say *please* when you asked for something. Likewise, our heavenly Father requires that what we ask of Him, we do so in the manner He tells us and with much thanksgiving. *Be careful for nothing; but in every thing by prayer and supplication with thanksgiving let your requests be made known unto God.* Philippians 5:6 As a child to a parent, there is a proper way to ask.

If we take a moment, clear our minds, and look at this from God's perspective, the answer becomes very clear.

There is a methodical approach to entering into God's Kingdom. The first thing is to understand how the Kingdom was established and the principles that govern the Kingdom of Heaven. Just as there are laws we must abide in our earthen life such as paying taxes, stopping at red lights, and so forth, there are also spiritual laws within the Kingdom of Heaven. When we become a born-again child of the Father, we are expected to know and follow the principles set forth by God. After all, they are meant for us. There is an orderly manner in approaching the Almighty King and not being privy to this knowledge will surely hinder receiving heavenly treasures and answered prayers.

In God's creation, we learn there is more than one heaven and one kingdom, but for our purpose at the moment we are focusing on the Almighty throne of God, His Kingdom of Heaven which encompasses all heavens and kingdoms. In studying how God established His Kingdom for man, we should concentrate on what is required to enter before His throne. God gives provisions for His children to be able to come before Him and receive blessings, gifts, and supernatural power for our spirit person. As He expects us to live a spirit life, His treasures are given to enable us to live, spiritually, within His Kingdom. This is how our Father protects and provides for His children while we remain in the physical world.

You may be surrounded by corruption, but once cleansed from the sin nature in Christ, it requires you learning how to live differently, spiritually. *Therefore we are buried with him by baptism into death: that like as Christ was raised up from the dead by the glory of the Father, even so we also should walk in newness of life.* Romans 6:4 You are born into the

Kingdom, the spirit realm of God and made a new creature (creation), cleansed of your unrighteousness, and prepared (made ready) to stand before your King, figuratively speaking, through your advocate, the Holy Spirit. *Therefore if any man be in Christ, he is a new creature: old things are passed away, behold, all things are become new.* 2 Corinthians 5:17 Your spirit birth is fresh, untouched of sin, like a newborn baby. This is exactly what you are to God at this very moment. A newborn baby, birthed in the Spirit of Christ, and handed over to the parent, God. Take a moment and meditate on the awesomeness of what has just transpired in Heaven; you are born into the spirit world of God. Angels in Heaven sing upon the spiritual birth of a born-again child.

Just as the natural birth of a baby brings forth gifts from family and friends, and as the wise men brought precious gifts to the newborn King, so your heavenly Father has a gift for you, His precious newborn child. God gives of Himself to live in your heart whereby He is always with you, and as you grow from an infant into maturity in His Word, there isn't anything He will not do for you. Just as you protect and provide for your children, so much more does God love, protect, and provide for His own.

The first thing God gives to you upon your spirit birth is the Comforter, the Holy Spirit, on the authority given in Christ. All things in Heaven have been given to the Son by the Father. *Jesus knowing that the Father had given all things into his hands, and that he was come from God, and went to God.* John 13:3 Therefore, we are given the Holy Ghost. *And I will pray the Father, and he shall give you another Comforter, that he may abide with you forever; Even the Spirit of truth; whom the world cannot receive, because it seeth him not, neither knoweth him: but ye know him; for he dwelleth with you, and shall be in you.* John 14:16-17

As the Holy Spirit was given to Christ's disciples to further His ministry, today in our spirit birth, we all receive the gift for all things of God come to us through the Holy Ghost. Though we remain with a soul in a physical body, our earnest desire is to grow our spirit person and mature in our knowledge of living a spirit life for the Father. This is the beginning of our eternal life.

Many fail to understand the significance of a birth into the Kingdom. We can only receive the storehouse of treasures in Heaven through the Holy Spirit on the authority given in Christ. Our soul and body are not capable of achieving this, and yet, we rely on our human skills to attempt entrance into the Kingdom. *Because the carnal mind is enmity against God: for it is not subject to the law of God, neither indeed can be. So then they that are in the flesh cannot please God.* Romans 8:7-8 God gives you the *key* to enter His Kingdom and that key is within the Holy Spirit. When you pray and a resolution is not forthcoming, it is not God withholding.

It is vital to learn how to appropriately apply the spiritual key that gains you entrance. *And I will give unto you the keys of the kingdom of heaven: and whatsoever thou shalt bind on earth shall be bound in heaven: and whatsoever thou shalt loose on earth shall be loosed in heaven.* Matthew 16:19 What this means is simply with your free will, you have control of your conduct, the natural versus the spirit.

Within your decision to apply your free will, spiritually,

you are capable of receiving the *keys of the Kingdom of Heaven* to *bind on earth and in heaven,* simultaneously, bringing forth into your earthen life the spiritual power for resolutions. There is a connection between heaven and earth, so that what you do in life reflects in the Kingdom, just as what you *loose* will also be witnessed in Heaven. If you don't do anything to secure heavenly treasures, then you are without: *loose on earth and shall be loosed in heaven.* They are lost to you. It is imperative to understand what is being taught in God's Word. Continuing to rely on your carnal nature rather than your spirit person, and not accepting there are two worlds, natural and spirit, will leave you empty-handed. Carnality cannot enter into the Kingdom; only the spirit, for the Kingdom of Heaven is a spiritual world.

God hears our prayers and knows our pleas. It saddens Him deeply to see our pain, sorrow, and suffering whether emotional or physical. However, He cannot change the precepts that He set at the foundation of His creation. Laws are in place and must be followed. *And be not conformed to this world: but be ye transformed by the renewing of your mind that ye may prove what is that good, and acceptable, and perfect will of God.* Romans 12:2 Everything God has done is for man, and we are responsible for our relationship with Him. If we falter, the fault is ours, not God.

Just as God gives man a *free will* to choose between a life of sin or a sinless life through a rebirth into the spirit realm, we should use our will to live as a spirit person. *It is sown a natural body; it is raised a spiritual body. There is a natural body, and there is a spiritual body.* 1 Corinthians 15:44 Always maintain emphasis on your spirit person and mature in knowledge and wisdom of God's Word, so that you may live a bountiful life in the Kingdom. Consider this analogy: if you travel to a foreign country without some knowledge and ability to speak their native language, it will be difficult to convey your request for ordering a meal, making a purchase, or for any accommodations. This holds true in living a spirit life to receive blessings, gifts, and supernatural power. You must know the language which is spiritual.

Knowing God is Spirit, it can only be in the spirit that we pray through the Holy Spirit to receive the magnificent gifts from the Father. Your *spirit*, through the *Holy Spirit* for the *Spirit of God* is the key to answered prayers.

Part II ~ The Gift

Let's step back to the basics for a moment. You are born a physical person, into a natural world. You grew up understanding the laws, or regulations, of how to live in society; what is acceptable conduct. You have a soul, your thoughts, which determines your personality and behavior and is influenced by the natural senses of what you see, hear, taste, touch, and smell. Now add an emotion such as happiness, sadness, anger, hurt, confusion, depression, laughter, fear, and so forth. When combining the physical senses with emotions, you are capable of making human decisions and choices. You completely understand this because you have been taught from birth. This is your natural life and normal to who you are as a person. Your soul governs the body and determines the decisions you make in life.

However, there is a third part of man and that is the spirit, for you are the trinity of body, soul, and spirit. The body and soul respond to the natural elements of this world, but there is a spirit within you that can only be awakened through a rebirth in Christ. Until such time you choose to be born into the spirit realm, the spirit cannot be called upon to perform any function in your daily life. The spirit within you is for a relationship with God and meant for eternity; therefore, your spirit only responds to the spirit realm. Upon your rebirth, the body becomes the temple for the Holy Spirit; and thus, it should be your spirit guided by the Holy Spirit in control of your soul and body. *What? Know ye not that your body is the temple of the Holy Ghost which is in you, which ye have of God, and ye are not your own?* 1 Corinthians 6:19 As you mature in God's Word, your spirit gains knowledge and wisdom to command your soul and body, meaning your decisions should be made according to your spirit and not your soul.

With the spirit rebirth in Christ, there are two worlds to consider; the natural and the spirit. Born into the natural you completely understand, born into the spirit you must learn. *That which is born of the flesh is flesh; and that which is born of the Spirit is spirit.* John 3:6 You accept the natural world; however, when you choose God, you acknowledge the spirit realm of His Kingdom. What occurs in the Kingdom is Christ gives you, a newborn infant, to the Father after you have been cleansed of sin through His Spirit. The Father, as a parent, has a gift for His infant child. This isn't any ordinary present, but one that enables you to have a relationship with Him, a continuous fellowship and communion.

Your gift of the Holy Spirit brings all things of God into your life, for the Holy Ghost is God. *Now we have received, not the spirit of the world, but the spirit which is God; that we might know the things that are freely given to us of God.* 1 Corinthians 2:12 Do you realize God is living on the inside of you in your heart? God is with you always, but do you acknowledge the magnitude of His presence? Most do not, which is unfortunate.

The Holy Spirit is revealed to man when God gives the Holy Ghost to His Son, Jesus. Upon His baptism in Jordan, the Holy Spirit descended from Heaven as a dove. *Behold my servant, whom I have chosen; my beloved, in whom my soul is well pleased: I will put my spirit upon him, and he shall show judgment to the Gentiles.* Matthew 12:18 Then Jesus gave the Comforter, the Holy Spirit, to His disciples. *And I will ask the Father, and He shall give you another Comforter, that he may abide with you for ever; Even the Spirit of truth; whom the world cannot receive, because it seeth him not, neither knoweth him: but ye know him; for he dwelleth with you, and shall be in you.* John 14:16-17 As God placed His Spirit upon His Son, and Christ sent the Holy Ghost to His disciples, so is the Holy Spirit given to you.

How can you expect to receive anything from someone you have never nurtured a relationship with? If God remains a stranger to you, and you ask for Him to supply for your needs, why should He respond when you've made no effort to know Him? God does provide because He established His blessings at the foundation of His creation, but our carnal or human efforts will not release the storehouse of treasures in Heaven. God has set forth the means He requires to come before Him. It must always be your *spirit* through the *Holy Spirit* to the *Spirit of God* to enter His *spiritual* Kingdom.

It is at this juncture that many remain lost to the blessings from the Father because they do not know they have a responsibility to a covenant they made in Christ when they asked to be born into the Kingdom. You may have thought your birth was solely for salvation, and if so, then you have missed the importance of your spirit birth. Salvation is given, but there is so much more that transpires. You agreed to a marriage in Christ for the Father when you ask to be born into His Kingdom. Not marrying God, but a commitment to Him in Christ. This is why when Christ returns for the saints, His bride, there will be a *Marriage Supper* in the Kingdom of Heaven before we live eternally with Christ as our Lord and King. *And he saith unto me, write, blessed are they which are called unto the marriage supper of the Lamb. And he saith unto me, These are the true sayings of God.* Revelation 19:9

Before Christ's death on the cross (Feast of Passover) and His resurrection (Feast of First Fruits), there was the ceremonial *Last Supper* with His chosen disciples. *And he took bread and gave thanks, and brake it, and gave unto them, saying, This is my body which is given for you: this do in remembrance of me. Likewise also the cup after supper, saying, This cup is the new testament in my blood, which is shed for you.* Luke 22:19-20 In Christ's second coming for His bride, the Marriage Supper is symbolic of the *official* joining of the children to the Father.

It is vital to understand that you are now a child of God with a commitment to live in the spirit, and in doing so, have access to everything of the Father which is given to you in Christ. This covenant is not an insignificant matter, but an eternal commitment. Just as in marriage to another person, you take vows to love, honor, and cherish one another, it is the same in your decision to be born in Christ for the Father. The initial gift of exchanging rings is a symbol of the bond to each other. As God has established the husband the head of the wife, he is to love her as God loves his church (children). This is not a reference that the wife is subservient to the husband, but rather an instruction from God telling man that for as much as He loves His children and cares for their needs, so is the husband to do the same. He is to protect, provide, and love her forever; *until death do us part.* Also, what the husband owns, she has entitlement of joint ownership. In this analogy, we can see the parallel of the components (love, protect, and provide) defining a natural marriage are the very same in our commitment to God, for God loves, protects, and provides with the gift of the Holy Spirit that binds us to Him.

Everything the Father has within His Kingdom, *home*, now belongs to His child, you. *For the Lord God is a sun and shield: the Lord will give grace and glory: no good thing will he withhold from them that walk uprightly.* Psalm 84:11 As a new creation in Christ, a newborn spirit person, you are prepared to live righteously, to *walk uprightly.* Christ gives you righteousness that you may be received by a holy Father.

You have salvation; however, if you are unaware of the significance of what transpired, then it becomes virtually impossible to communicate with your heavenly Father. The relationship must be nurtured in continuous fellowship and rely on the gift God gives you. We are not privileged to go directly before the Almighty King as we remain in carnality, but He provides a spokesperson who can. *He therefore that despiseth, despiseth not man, but God, who hath also given unto us his Holy Spirit.* 1 Timothy 4:8 Notice: *who hath also given unto us his Holy Spirit;* God gives Himself as the Holy Spirit to live in your heart and be with you always. This is powerful! *Who hath also sealed us, and given the earnest of the Spirit in our hearts.* 2 Corinthians 1:22 He is your *key* to everything within God's Kingdom, for all things of the Father come to you through the Holy Spirit. *The blessing of the Lord, it maketh rich, and he addeth no sorrow with it.* Proverbs 10:22 God has so much to give to you and deeply desires for a relationship and daily communion with His beloved child. It is unimaginable that anyone would not want this intimate relationship with their heavenly Father.

Your fellowship with God begins with your desire to have a relationship with Him, to learn of His nature, to accept His Kingdom principles, and to allow the Holy Spirit to teach you all things of the Father. *For they that are after the flesh do mind the things of the flesh; but they that are after the Spirit the things of the Spirit.* Romans 8:5 Your spirit is *alive* waiting for instructions, eager to grow from infancy to adulthood within the spirit realm. Your spirit knows the Holy Spirit is in your heart, but if your soul keeps Him at a distance and you never communicate with Him, then your spirit person doesn't have an opportunity to grow up, and unfortunately, remains an infant without knowledge. Don't find yourself disconnected, a broken link to the Kingdom wandering aimlessly without the guidance of the Holy Spirit.

Your heavenly Father has treasures within His Kingdom that are literally at your disposal for a better life today, but He expects you to mature in your spirit, so that His spiritual gifts may be given to you when you ask for them. *Likewise the Spirit also helpeth our infirmities: for we know not what we should pray for as we ought: but the Spirit itself maketh intercession for us with groanings which cannot be uttered.* Romans 8:26 All things of the Father are *gifts* and all things we desire from the Father must be *asked*. The responsibility in receiving spiritual gifts is in you diligently learning to live spiritually. This is why carnal prayers do not render an answer from God. *Which things also we speak, not in the words which man's wisdom teacheth, but which the Holy Ghost teacheth; comparing spiritual things with spiritual.* 1 Corinthians 2:13 Prayers will remain unanswered simply because of our lack of knowledge of the fellowship we must have with God through the Holy Spirit. If the relationship is not nurtured, then the communion doesn't exist. It is that simple and that profound.

It appears evident that religious doctrines fail miserably in teaching of the Holy Spirit. If they did, there would be more believers receiving answered prayers which raises the question: Why are they not helping newborn believers to learn of the Trinity of God; and thus, the laws that govern God's Kingdom? Perhaps, because they were never taught themselves; after all, you can't teach something you don't know. *Beware lest any man spoil you through philosophy and vain deceit, after the tradition of men, after the rudiments of the world, and not after Christ.* Colossians 2:8 Man passes traditions and doctrines down through generations and holds them as truth. The teaching of the Holy Spirit is blindly withheld, or purposefully glazed over in our congregations because of a lack of knowledge in the very individuals professing the Word of God.

It is the greatest deception embedded within religion that specifically prevents you from the knowledge of the *power* that is within you. We listen to the teachings of man and not the Word of God. *Making the word of God of none effect through your tradition, which ye have delivered: and many such like things do ye.* Mark 7:13 There is absolutely no way the ruler of this world, Satan, would want you to have a relationship with the Almighty King and gain all the magnificent gifts and supernatural power He has for you. It is a block to prevent you from connecting to God and is done deliberately and specifically through the lack of teaching of the Holy Spirit. Remember, ALL Kingdom power comes through the Holy Spirit.

When you have the Holy Spirit, you have God *living* within you who is the *key* to His Kingdom, literally. *In whom ye also trusted, after ye heard the word of truth, the gospel of your salvation: in whom also after that ye believed, ye were sealed with the Holy Spirit of promise.* Ephesians 1:13 Satan doesn't want you to know how to acquire entrance and gain supernatural power that you can use today to deflect his wiles. He wants to keep you as far from God's truth as possible, so that you fail in this life. Remember, the Holy Spirit is the Spirit of Truth and is the ONLY way to the throne of God. *Even the Spirit of Truth; whom the world cannot receive, because it seeth him not, neither knoweth him: but ye know him; for he dwelleth with you, and shall be in you.* John 14:17

It doesn't change your salvation in Christ; however, it most certainly prevents you from succeeding in receiving answered prayers, or a healing, or whatever you may need. Satan's focus is always to steal, kill, and destroy. He will steer you away from your heavenly Father and destroy that which He can in your life easily under the disguise of *lack of knowledge*. The ONLY preventive measure is in your personal gift, the Holy Spirit. One of the numerous responsibilities of the Holy Spirit is to protect you from these attacks. You have a personal defender, the Holy Spirit, who is your Father, but do you know that? He is within you ready to defend and deflect, protecting you always if you depend on

Him. Think of the Holy Spirit as your personal bodyguard.

Let it sink into your soul this most precious knowledge: the Holy Spirit is your *key* to a relationship and communion with your heavenly Father and entrance into His Almighty Kingdom. This is worth repeating! He is available 24/7 to provide and protect you. *And he that searcheth the hearts knoweth what is the mind of the Spirit, because he maketh intercession for the saints according to the will of God.* Romans 8:27 Upon receiving the Holy Spirit after your spirit birth in Christ, it is mandatory to quicken or awaken (baptism) the Holy Spirit. *But if the Spirit of him that raised up Jesus from the dead dwell in you, he that raised up Christ from the dead shall also quicken your mortal bodies by his Spirit that dwelleth in you.* Romans 8:11

You have received the gift; however, you must awaken the gift with a prayer of acknowledgment. Here's an analogy that may help. If someone gives you a bank card as a gift, and you hold onto it without calling the number on the back to activate the card, but instead place it in your wallet, or throw it into a drawer, there are no benefits from the gift. The card is useless in making purchases. Likewise, this is true of the Holy Spirit. You have the gift, but are not applying the benefits in your life.

As your spirit is asleep until given a birth in Christ; thus, the Holy Spirit is asleep until you acknowledge His presence. Christ awakens you, and you in turn awaken the Holy Spirit. All it takes is praying to the Father that you accept His gift and ask that the Holy Spirit be actively present in your life. It's that simple. *Father, thank you for sending your Son to free me from the bondage of sin, and as I am reborn in*

Christ, I am also thankful for the gift of the Holy Spirit. I come before you asking that the Holy Ghost be awakened within me, so that I may live and serve according to your Word. On the name of Christ and the blood He shed at Calvary for me, I pray, Amen. Begin your spirit life with a heartfelt desire to love your Father and want a relationship with Him. Live according to His Kingdom principles and accept the presence of the Holy Spirit, so that all things within the Kingdom of Heaven may be given to you when you pray. When you approach the Father in the manner He has established, your prayers will be answered, He promises it!

The first lesson as a newborn spirit person is the Holy Spirit removes the veil (parables) that you may read the Father's Words with spiritual eyes and learn of Him and His Kingdom. As an infant, your spiritual tutor will teach you all things of the spirit realm. *And he said unto them, Unto you it is given to know the mystery of the kingdom of God: but unto them that are without, all these things are done in parables: That seeing they may see, and not perceive; and hearing they may hear, and not understand; lest at any time they should be converted, and their sins should be forgiven them.* Mark 4:11-12 Words of God are solely for His children and this is why the Holy Spirit is also referred to as the Spirit of Truth.

The Holy Spirit is your best friend, confidant, protector, provider, and advocate (spokesperson) before God. He is the most valuable *person* in your life, for now you have His supernatural provisions in your natural life. *Which things also we speak, not in the words which man's wisdom teacheth, but which the Holy Ghost teacheth; comparing spiritual things with spiritual.* 1 Corinthians 2:13 With a steadfast trust in the Holy Spirit, the communication *channel* is open to you, so that you may pray to the Father and the Father will answer through the Holy Spirit. *Now the God of hope fill you with all joy and peace in believing, that ye may abound in hope, through the power of the Holy Ghost.* Romans 15:13 Believe in the friendship of the Holy Spirit and see Him as a person you can depend on; a best friend who is with you always looking out for your best interest. Spend time with Him conversing as you would with a dear friend.

Just as in friendship, you would not knowingly cause harm or grief, be cautious to not grieve the Holy Spirit. Don't allow soulful thoughts to interfere with your relationship with your best friend. *And grieve not the Holy Spirit of God, whereby ye are sealed unto the day of redemption.* Ephesians 4:30 To know the things that fall into this category, the Holy Spirit tells us what He expects in our relationship with Him, so that we do not unbeknown grieve His presence. *That ye put off concerning the former conversation the old man, which is corrupt according to the deceitful lusts; And be renewed in the spirit of your mind; And that you put on the new man, which after God is created in righteousness and true holiness. Wherefore putting away lying, speaking every man truth with his neighbor: for we are members one of another. Be ye angry, and sin not: let not the sun go down upon your wrath: Neither give place to the devil. Let him that stole steal no more: but let him labour, working with his hands the thing which is good, that he may have to give to him that needeth. Let no corrupt communication proceed out of your mouth, but that which is good to the use of edifying, that it may minister grace unto the hearers. Let all bitterness, and wrath, and anger, and clamour, and evil speaking be put away from you, with all malice: And be ye kind one to another, tenderhearted, forgiving one another, even as God for Christ's sake hath forgiven you.* Ephesians 4:22-29; 31-32

We are to be mindful to live with the *Fruits of the Spirit* which are the Holy Spirit's requirements as He lives in our heart and not allow sin such as lying, stealing, anger, bitterness and so forth to influence our mind and conduct. Just as you would not deliberately upset a friend, you surely must be conscientious to not grieve God.

Choose to live a life for the Father within His Kingdom. Though born in Christ, if you fail to *crossover* from the carnal to a spirit life, you miss out on the precious heavenly gifts, healing, and supernatural power. Therefore, if you walk away from your birth into the spiritual world, knowingly or unbeknown, you cannot rightfully expect to receive Kingdom treasures and supernatural power, for these are solely for the spirit person.

It is so much more than having salvation; it is everything God has to give to you right now, today, but it requires learning to live in two worlds simultaneously and allowing your spirit to excel over your soul in all matters of life. It's living in the Kingdom!

Part III ~ The Trinity

In any relationship there is mutual admiration, respect, and love from both individuals. This is defined as eros love in a marriage, storge love of parents for their children, and the affectionate love in friendship is philia. We know God's love is agape, an unconditional love. God's enduring love is expressed in His Trinity of the Father, Son, and Holy Ghost; His love for man with the trinity of body, soul, and spirit; and His Almighty Kingdom functions with mercy, grace, and faith. It is noteworthy that three trinities have within them respectively three presentations.

In the beginning God created the heaven and the earth begins our study of the foundation of God's creation. In the generations captured in the Old Testament, we have the history of God's relationship with His chosen people, the Israelites. There is the foretelling of a shadow of things to come (Christ) as acknowledged in the Feasts, witnessing the establishment of His Covenants, prophecies of His timeline and the events therein. In the New Testament, we have God leaving His throne and coming to earth as Christ to provide a means that His children may return to Him for an eternal life, salvation is taught.

Let's begin with the Trinity of God. As just stated, God presents Himself to man as revealed in the Father, the Son, and the Holy Ghost. God is all three, so why is it necessary to have three separate personages of Himself? Why not simply be God, our heavenly Father, and leave it at that? Because each has a very specific purpose for man's life; each gives to man separately the requirements for a relationship with the Father, from being born into the spirit realm (Christ), to entrance within the spirit Kingdom (Holy Spirit) while continuing to live in the natural world. Your eternal spirit life begins the moment of your birth in Christ, and only in your commitment to learn how to live in the spirit do you have a communion with God. It begins with God and comes full circle; from the Father, through Christ and the Holy Spirit to God.

It is important to understand the purpose for each. For example, praying to be born into the spirit realm through the Holy Spirit will not give you a rebirth into the Kingdom. That is specifically the role of Christ. To pray to Christ for a healing or miracle does not render an answer because this is not provided through Christ once He returned to the Kingdom. *By His stripes ye are healed* applies to the action of what Christ did for man; however, to receive the healing He provided upon His death at Calvary, we must rely on the Holy Spirit. Healing is granted on Christ's *authority* but *received* through the Holy Spirit.

When Christ was on earth, He did everything as One because He had the Holy Ghost within Him. However, after ascending to the Kingdom of Heaven, everything comes to man through Christ *and* the Holy Spirit. Can you begin to understand why God established the Trinity. Each is God, but each has a definitive purpose in man's life. You have to know Christ and the Holy Spirit and their gifts, so that you have knowledge of how to acquire spiritual gifts within the Kingdom. If you are unaware of the significance of God's presentation of Himself, your salvation is not affected; however, you miss out on everything God has for you. There is a trinity to God, to man, and to the Kingdom. It is vital to our spirit life to know this.

In the gifts of the Trinity, we learn that God and Christ's gifts are *administration* and *ministry* while the Holy Ghost's gifts are of *power*. It is imperative to understand the gifts each presents for man's life, for there is a reason it is established this way. *Now concerning spiritual gifts brethren, I would not have you ignorant.* 1 Corinthians 12:1 And, *Now there are diversities of gifts, but the same Spirit. And there are differences of administrations, but the same Lord. And there are diversities of operations, but it is the same God which worketh all in all.* 1 Corinthians 12:4-6 God's gifts are administrative and all encompassing in the function of His Kingdom which are apostles, prophets, teachers, healing, miracles, helps, governments, and diversities of tongues. *Now ye are the body of Christ, and members in particular. And God hath set some in the church, first apostles, secondarily prophets, thirdly teachers, after that miracles, then gifts of healings, helps, governments, diversities of tongues. Are all apostles? Are all prophets? are all teachers? are all workers of miracles? Have all the gifts of healing? do all speak with tongues? do all interpret? But covet earnestly the best gifts: and yet show I unto you a more excellent way.* 1 Corinthians 12:27-31 We can see the inclusion of the gifts of Christ and the Holy Spirit within God's gifts. God appoints His gifts through the Holy Spirit.

God came to earth as the second person of the Trinity, Christ, with a specific purpose to fulfill. Upon His physical birth, He was already acknowledged as a King from another world. *And when he was twelve years old, they went up to Jerusalem after the custom of the feast. And when they had fulfilled the days, as they returned, the child Jesus tarried behind in Jerusalem; and Joseph and his mother knew not it.* Luke 2:42-43 *And it came to pass, that after three days they found him in the temple, sitting in the midst of the doctors, both hearing them, and asking them questions. And all that heard him were astonished at his understanding and answers.* Luke 2:46-47

When His parents found Him in the temple, they were astonished where He was and amazed at the knowledge He spoke. Can you imagine this scene; here's a young boy who typically would not have permission to be in the temple, nor to have the privilege of a conversation with prominent people, and yet, there He sat amongst them conversing with a greater intellect than their own. When they questioned their son, Jesus replied to them: *And he said unto them, How is it that ye sought me? Wist ye not that I must be about my Father's business? And they understood not the saying which he spoke unto them.* Luke 2:49-50

Upon their return to Nazareth, Jesus' wisdom grew. *And Jesus increased in wisdom and stature, and in favour with God and man.* Luke 2:52 We do not have an account of how Jesus spent His years from age twelve to thirty before His baptism with the Holy Ghost. We do know His knowledge and wisdom increased, for He received *favour with God and man*. It is logical to assume that Jesus did not keep knowledge to Himself, but often conversed with prominent people of His day as He did in the temple in Jerusalem. It would appear that His teaching ministry truly began on that day He stayed behind, and the place Christ will return as our King to the sacred temple in Jerusalem.

When Christ was baptized by John the Baptist in Jordan, He received the Holy Ghost and it was after His baptism that He began openly teaching of the Kingdom of God and performing miracles and healing. *And it came to pass in those days, that Jesus came from Nazareth of Galilee, and was baptized of John in Jordan. And straightway coming up out of the water, he saw the heavens opened, and the Spirit like a dove descending upon him: And there came a voice from heaven, saying, Thou art my beloved Son, in whom I am well pleased.* Mark 1:9-11 We learn in the Scriptures that Jesus was the age of thirty when He taught to the multitude who gathered around Him. *And Jesus himself began to be about thirty years of age (as was supposed) the son of Joseph, which was the son of Heli.* Luke 3:23

His first miracle was at the wedding in Cana when He changed water to wine. *This beginning of miracles did Jesus in Cana in Galilee, and manifested forth his glory, and his disciples believed on him.* John 2:11 As an adult, His ministry lasted three years once He received the power of the Holy Ghost. It is noteworthy that even Jesus did not perform miracles, healing, or teach of the Kingdom of Heaven until after He received the Holy Ghost. This holds true today of the importance of the Holy Spirit in our lives. As supernatural heavenly power came to the man, Jesus, from the Father, so today the same Holy Spirit comes to you. We can see the relevancy for the Holy Spirit in our life.

God came to earth in Christ to be the Good Shepherd gathering the flock (lost children through sin) and enable them to have a means of returning to their heavenly Father. He performed miracles and healing to prove His truth. Christ knew to remove the sins from the physical man, He would need to be like them, of flesh; and thus, bore the sins and transgressions of this earthen world upon His own body on the cross at Calvary. *For Christ also hath once suffered for sins, the just for the unjust, that he might bring us to God, being put to death in the flesh, but quickened by the Spirit.* 1 Peter 3:18 All iniquities and infirmities were destroyed, *put to death*, on the cross in Jesus.

When Christ was *quickened by the Spirit* (resurrection) and returned to the Kingdom, He provided three specific benefits for man: first, our spirit birth through His Spirit; second, He gives us the gift of grace; and third, He gives His authority that we may call upon heavenly powers. As Christ sits at the right hand of the Father, all things within the Kingdom are authorized for man through Him. Everything comes through the *authority* in Christ, which is not the same thing to say that everything is *provided* by Christ.

Though at first it may appear to be a contradiction in terms; however, if we study the purpose of the Trinity of God, then we see the methodology for His creation. Thus, all things we receive are from God, the Father, authorized through Christ, the Son, and given by the Holy Spirit.

It is imperative to differentiate between the purpose of Christ and the purpose of the Holy Spirit. The authority is in Christ for the Father has given all things in the Kingdom and on earth to the Son; however, the Holy Spirit is given for a *relationship* with God which begins with the teaching of His Word. All the magnificent gifts and supernatural power within the Kingdom are provided through the Holy Spirit. This is an important lesson; authority and provision. If you are praying and expecting Christ to answer, this is not His role in your life.

Christ's gifts are ministerial which are apostles, prophets, evangelists, pastors, and teachers. *Now that he ascended, what is it but that he also descended first into the lower parts of the earth? He that descended is the same also that ascended up far above all heavens, that he might fill all things. And he gave some, apostles; and some, prophets; and some, evangelists; and some, pastors and teachers; For the perfecting of the saints, for the work of the ministry, for the edifying of the body of Christ.* Ephesians 4:9-12 Therefore, if your dependance on Christ is for answered prayers, you can see that His gifts are not provisional. They are for the continuation of His ministry that began on earth. Though we have many doctrines, pastors, preachers, priests, and theologians today, it does not mean they are all called by Christ to continue His ministry.

There are many professing the Word of God who have not been anointed by Christ. However, once you have the truth of God's Word as deciphered through the Holy Spirit, you are able to recognize false teachings. It is our responsibility as saints to be disciples just as Christ's disciples went forth after His death once anointed with the Holy Spirit. With the Spirit of Truth teaching all things of the Kingdom, our profession will be in His truth.

When we address the third person of the Trinity of God,

the Holy Spirit, we learn His purpose is to unite us to our heavenly Father in communion. The Holy Spirit is our spiritual tutor, our advocate before our Almighty King, and provides the supernatural treasures within the Kingdom; He protects and provides. Just as you are a parent who gives gifts to your children, so does our heavenly Father have gifts for you. *If ye then, being evil know how to give good gifts unto your children: how much more shall your heavenly Father give the Holy Spirit to them that ask him?* Luke 11:13 The Holy Spirit has many provisions and gives the most gifts which are wisdom, knowledge, faith, healing, miracles, prophecy, discerning of spirits, speaking in tongues, and interpretation of tongues. In the Holy Spirit, God has provided all that you will need for your spirit life. *But the manifestation of the Spirit is given to every man to profit withal. For to one is given by the Spirit the word of wisdom; to another the word of knowledge by the same Spirit; To another faith by the same Spirit; to another the gifts of healing by the same Spirit; To another the working of miracles; to another prophecy; to another discerning of spirits; to another divers kinds of tongues; to another the interpretation of tongues: But all these work that one and the selfsame Spirit, dividing to every man severally as he will.* 1 Corinthians 12:7-11

Notice faith, healing, miracles, wisdom, and knowledge are all given through the Holy Spirit. There is nothing lacking in what you may receive through His provisions. *Again, the kingdom of heaven is like unto treasure hid in a field; the which when a man hath found, he hideth, and for joy thereof goeth and selleth all that he hath, and buyeth that field.* Matthew 13:44 Can you begin to see the magnificent beauty of how God set everything within His Kingdom for you? It is the most awesome love story ever told, for it is all about you, the subject of His desires. God wants to fellowship with you, today and every day. In your trust and reliance on the Holy Spirit, you can expect answers to your prayers, for God provided it at the foundation of His creation and promises it!

Once we understand the Trinity of God is for man, there are requirements of the Holy Spirit that we abide in. These are referred to as the *Fruits of the Spirit* which are love, joy, peace, longsuffering, gentleness, goodness, faith, meekness, and temperance. *But the fruit of the Spirit is love, joy, peace, longsuffering, gentleness, goodness, faith, meekness, temperance: against such there is no law.* Galatians 5:22-23 When we renew our thinking, we replace the carnal negative emotions of anger, hate, disillusionment, disappointment, fear, and so on with the Fruits of the Holy Spirit. In our heart we have peace, joy, love, faith, goodness, kindness, and so forth. With these fruits, we conduct our behavior. Think of it as new management who has brought new guidelines into the operation of a business. In this case, you are the new creation in Christ, and the Holy Spirit is the new management with His expectations.

Though you have been born in Christ for a relationship with the Father, it requires your continuous fellowship through the Holy Spirit for a true commitment to God. If you are not living a spirit to Spirit life daily, then the very lack in the fellowship with God is a position of taking Him for granted; to only call upon Him in time of need. Those who fall within this category probably don't even realize that they are doing so, but if they are believing minimally of His provisions and doubt His abilities to give, then the relationship is not intimate with the Father; thus, there is a void (disconnect) in fellowship with Him. The benefits of the relationship can only occur with our firm commitment. *If ye abide in me, and my words abide in you, ye shall ask what ye will, and it shall be done unto you.* John 15:7 Your relationship can only be as trustworthy as you have faith in Christ and the Holy Spirit. Remember, you can have an awareness of God and Christ, but not be a recipient of Kingdom benefits. You are responsible for the lack of God's greatest in your life. This may sound harsh, but nevertheless, it is God's reality.

As we understand the trinity of God, and the trinity of man, there is also the trinity of the Kingdom. This is referring to the functionality of the Kingdom of Heaven which is mercy, grace, and faith. Just as we learn to understand the nature of God, His creation, and His love, we should also give attention to comprehending the laws that govern His Kingdom. Each country has a parliament or governmental structure as does the Kingdom of Heaven. Beginning with mercy, we may consider it the platform, or base that grace and faith come forth from. *But God, who is rich in mercy, for his great love wherewith he loved us.* Ephesians 2:4 Consider the soil when you plant a seed, and the seed grows into a plant. Perhaps, mercy can be likened to the soil, for God's mercy is present no matter the disobedience of His people. Mercy has always been at the forefront of God's Kingdom.

Webster's dictionary defines mercy as the compassionate or kindly forbearance shown towards an offender, an enemy, or other person under one's influences; an act of kindness or favor, something that gives evidence of divine favor; blessing. This is precisely what God gives to man. In His love, we experience His mercy. Just like the mercy that is given to a prodigal child who has strayed, the love always remains. It was mercy God gave to the Israelites in their disobedience when He removed them from bondage in Egypt. *Thou in thy mercy hast led forth the people which though hast redeemed: thou hast guided them in thy strength unto thy holy habitation.* Exodus 15:13 Without God's mercy, how would we experience grace and faith? *And he said, I will make all my goodness pass before thee, and I will proclaim the name of the Lord before thee; and will be gracious to whom I will be gracious, and will show mercy on whom I will show mercy.* Exodus 33:19

It is within God's mercy we witness the true expression of His love. God's mercy never changes and is for the saved and unsaved because it is established within His Kingdom as the foundation for grace and faith. *Not by works of righteousness we have done, but according to his mercy he saved us, by the washing of regeneration, and renewing of the Holy Ghost.* Titus 3:5 Without God's mercy, man would not exist. It is His compassion for mankind.

An analogy to living in the mercy of God is likened to an insurance policy; however, there is no better life insurance, health coverage, or retirement benefits than with God. His provisions never expire, and we are guaranteed physical and emotional healing, provided prosperity, and given eternal life. We are far greater than the angels, for we are God's children. *Keep yourselves in the love of God, looking for the mercy of our Lord Jesus Christ unto eternal life.* Jude 1:21 God's mercy is the love and patience He expresses continuously to man. His mercy is constant without degree or dimension. It is always in place, a perfect expression of love. *For the Lord is good; his mercy is everlasting; and his truth endureth to all generations.* Psalm 100:5 To have mercy or compassion towards someone who has done an injustice is a remarkable act of kindness. God shows mercy towards a sinful people.

Once we understand the mercy of God upon all His creation, then grace is evident. Grace is a gift of pardon and forgiveness. Grace existed in the generations within the Old Testament era, for grace is of the Kingdom, and as God extended His mercy, He also gave grace (forgiveness). There is the example of Noah and Moses. *But Noah found grace in the eyes of the Lord.* Genesis 6:8 Also, *And the Lord said unto Moses, I will do this thing also that thou hast spoken: for thou hast found grace in my sight, and I know thee by name.* Exodus 33:17 God had a covenant with both Noah and Moses. He showed grace to those who were faithful to Him. With the new covenant in Christ, grace is freely given to all who believe. *For the law was given to Moses, but grace and truth came by Jesus Christ.* John 1:17 Also, *Grace be with you, mercy, and peace, from God the Father, and from the Lord Jesus Christ, the Son of the Father, in truth and love.* 2 John 1:3 However, we can fall out of grace through sin. God does not remove grace from our life, but we can remove ourselves from the influences of grace.

So many precious gifts from the Father through His Son and the Holy Spirit are all for you. It is because of grace that we may acquire God's many gifts. *But unto every one of us is given grace according to the measure of the gift of Christ.* Ephesians 4:7 In remembering that all things of the Father are gifts to His children, we receive grace as a gift. Grace is very special in our lives because forgiveness is within grace. As Christ removes our sins and sinful nature, we are given grace, pardoned of sin, that we may be acceptable to God. *Being justified freely by his grace through the redemption that is in Christ Jesus.* Romans 3:24 This is not a free ticket to sin and receive forgiveness knowingly, but rather that should we slip in our carnal lives and commit an act that grieves God, we may be forgiven when we acknowledge our misconduct and ask forgiveness.

Just as you would forgive your child for a disobedience, so does our heavenly Father forgive our trespasses. *For sin shall not have dominion over you: for ye are not under the law, but under grace.* Romans 6:14 Again, take note of the terminology: *but under grace.* Simply stated: upon your birth into the Kingdom of Heaven, you are living in grace. Grace is always in the Kingdom, but sin keeps you from grace until you repent. *I thank my God always on your behalf, for the grace of God is given you by Jesus Christ.* 1 Corinthians 1:4 With our Father's mercy and grace, we live in faith to His Word. Though faith is a gift, faith is our part, for mercy and grace are given by God, but faith reveals our trust in Him.

The third part of the trinity is faith. Interesting how faith begets grace. As we live spiritually within the Kingdom, we know it is the gift of faith that enables us to have a relationship with God and to receive His blessings in our life. Accepting that God's mercy and grace is upon His children, so must our faith be just as prevalent towards our Father. *Without faith it is impossible to please God.* Hebrews 11:6 It should become our desire to be an obedient child with wisdom in our Father's Word. In doing so, we gain knowledge of how to walk by faith. *For by grace are ye saved through faith; and that not of yourselves: it is the gift of God: Not of works, lest any man should boast.* Ephesians

2:8-9 God's loving and forgiving nature as shown in His mercy (compassion) with grace (forgiveness) is fulfilled in faith. *By whom also we have access by faith into this grace wherein we stand, and rejoice in hope of the glory of God.* Romans 5:2 It is important to know the semantics of how our faith releases grace into our lives, *by our faith into this grace.* Though mercy and grace are foundational within the Kingdom, it is our faith that secures grace.

An analogy would be likened to a cell phone. If we have not taken the time to read the manual that came with the new device, but instead continue to operate the phone based on our perception of how it works, we can miss many of its features. Just because we haven't made ourselves privy to various preprogrammed applications, doesn't mean they aren't accessible on the phone. Same holds true with faith. We receive the gift and are expected to study the manual, the Bible, to learn how faith operates in the Kingdom, so we will not be without the many blessings that come through faith.

It is important to know how to allocate faith to release grace like a combination to a lock. *Let us therefore come boldly unto the throne of grace that we may obtain mercy, and find grace to help in time of need.* Hebrews 4:16 God's grace is omnipresent, but we can obstruct its function in our life. Faith is much more than simply believing God is your heavenly Father, it is the *spiritual language* by which we have access to the Kingdom of Heaven. Through faith, our trust is solely expressed within our spirit for the Spirit of God. Remember, it is a spiritual relationship with the Father; therefore, it is how we conduct our spirit life that matters.

God, your Almighty King, requires that when you ask to

be born into His Kingdom and become His child, you acknowledge the importance of your request. In your spirit birth, you accept a covenant in Christ, and the gift of the Holy Spirit. You desire to live by His Kingdom principles and allow the Fruits of the Holy Spirit to abide in your heart and be the guidepost of your daily behavior. You want an intimate fellowship with your Father and trust Him implicitly. As you mature in knowledge and wisdom of God and His Kingdom, you give thanksgiving and glory always to your Father for the blessings He bestows upon your life as you live *spirit* to His *Spirit* within the *spiritual* Kingdom of Heaven. Praise, glory, honor, and thanksgiving to God, our Almighty King! Amen

Summary

In summary, it is imperative to understand that when you accept God as your heavenly Father and Christ, His Son, you are committing to a new and better covenant given in Christ. You are joined to Christ in Spirit, married to Him through a covenant. Without living accordingly, you miss the blessings such as unanswered prayers. Each believer must fulfill his commitment in their relationship with Christ. Christ fulfills His, and you are to do the same as in any marriage. *Wherefore my brethren, ye also are become dead to the law by the body of Christ: that ye should be <u>married to another, even to him who is raised from the dead</u>, that we should bring forth fruit unto God. For when we were in the flesh, the motions of sins, which were by law, did the work in our members to bring forth fruit unto death. But now we are delivered from the law, that being dead wherein we were held: that we should serve in newness of spirit, and not in the oldness of the letter.* Romans 7:4-6

In Christ's first appearance on earth in the flesh, He had the Last Supper with His disciples before His crucifixion. Born into the spirit realm, you become the bride of Christ. When He returns a second time to earth for His bride, there will be a Marriage Supper that *officially* unites you to the Father. However, becoming a bride of Christ begins the day you accept Him and your spirit is entwined with His Spirit; you are joined.

Within this marriage, Christ gives you gifts. Some occur because of His sacrifice at Calvary and others are given to His bride, today. We know of redemption (cleansed of iniquities), salvation (eternal life), righteousness, grace (forgiveness), and the Holy Spirit have been given to each new believer. *But unto every one of us is given grace according to the measure of the gift of Christ.* Ephesians 4:7 As His bride and joint-heir within the Kingdom, you also receive Christ's authority; therefore, what Christ owns also belongs to you. *The Spirit itself beareth witness with our spirit, that we are the children of God: And if children, then heirs; heirs of God, and joint-heirs with Christ; if so be that we suffer with him, that we may be also glorified together.* Romans 8:16-17

Thus, whatever you ask giving glory to the Father shall be given to you. The treasures within the storehouse are for you and Christ gives you the keys to the Kingdom that you may obtain what you need for your earthen life. *And I will give you the keys of the kingdom of heaven: and whatsoever thou shall bind on earth shall be bound in heaven: and whatsoever thou shalt loose on earth shall be loosed in heaven.* Matthew 16:19 Nothing is withheld from you, for you are married to Christ.

It is God's will to give to His children. We are to know that He delights in doing so, for we have the knowledge of understanding His will in our lives. *It is written, Eye hath not seen, nor ear heard, neither have entered into the heart of man, the things which God hath prepared for them that love him. But God hath revealed them unto us by his Spirit: for the Spirit searcheth all things, yea, the deep things of God. For what man knoweth the things of a man, save the spirit of man which is in him? Even so the things of God knoweth no man, but the Spirit of God. Now we have received, not the spirit of the world, but the spirit which is of God; that we might know the things that are freely given to us of God. Which things also we speak, not in the words which man's wisdom teacheth, but which the Holy Ghost teacheth: comparing spiritual things with spiritual.* 1 Corinthians 2:9-13

We must understand the significance of our commitment to Christ for our relationship with God when we asked to be born into the Spirit Kingdom. Our lack of knowledge leaves us paralyzed in living a spiritual life and receiving the supernatural gifts the Father has provided. All things are possible with God, provided through the Holy Spirit, and given when you dedicate to living a spiritual life in marriage to Christ. On Christ's authority through the Holy Spirit will your prayers be answered.

Scriptures

Matthew 13:44 *Again, the kingdom of heaven is like unto treasure hid in a field; the which when a man hath found, he hideth, and for joy thereof goeth and selleth all that he hath, and buyeth that field.*

Romans 8:26 *Likewise the spirit also helpeth our infirmities: for we know not what we should pray for as we ought: but the spirit itself maketh intercession for us with groanings which cannot be uttered.*

1 Corinthians 6:20 *For ye are bought with a price: therefore glorify God in your body, and in your spirit, which are God's.*

1 Corinthians 2:12 *Now we have received, not the spirit of the world, but the spirit which is of God; that we might know the things that are freely given to us of God.*

1 Corinthians 3:18-19 *Let no man deceive himself. If any man among you seemeth to be wise in this world, let him become a fool, that he may be wise. For the wisdom of this world is foolishness with God. For it is written, He taketh the wise in their own craftiness.*

John 4:24 *God is a spirit and they that worship him must worship him in spirit and in truth.*

John 14:16-17 *And I will pray the Father, and he shall give you another Comforter, that he may abide with you for ever; Even the Spirit of truth, whom the world cannot receive, because it seeth him not, neither knoweth him: but ye know him; for he dwelleth with you and shall be in you.*

John 14:26 *But the Comforter, which is the Holy Ghost, whom the Father will send in my mane, he shall teach you all things, and bring all things to your remembrance, whatsoever I have said unto you.*

John 15:26 *But when the Comforter is come, whom I will send unto you from the Father, even the Spirit of truth, which proceeedeth from the Father, he shall testify of me.*

John 16:7 *Nevertheless I tell you the truth; It is expedient for you that I go away: for if I go not away, the Comforter will not come unto you; but if I depart, I will send him unto you.*

John 16:13 *Howbeit when he, the Spirit of truth, is come, he will guide you into all truth: for he shall not speak of himself, but whatsoever he shall hear, that shall he speak and he will show you things to come.*

Matthew 6:33 *But seek ye first the kingdom of God, and his righteousness; and all these things shall be added unto you.*

Hebrews 10:16-17 *This is the covenant that I will make with them after those days, saith the Lord, I will put my laws into their hearts, and in their minds will I write them; And their sins and iniquities will I remember no more.*

1 Corinthians 4:20 *For the kingdom of God is not in word, but in power.*

Ephesians 2:4 *But God, who is rich in mercy, for his great love wherewith he loved us.*

Psalm 100:5 *For the Lord is good; his mercy is everlasting; and his truth endureth to all generations.*

Jude 1:21 *Keep yourselves in the love of God, looking for the mercy of our Lord Jesus Christ unto eternal life.*

1 Chronicles 16:34 *O' give thanks unto the Lord; for he is good; for his mercy endureth for ever.*

2 John 1:3 *Grace be with you, mercy, and peace, from God the Father, and from the Lord Jesus Christ, the Son of the Father, in truth and love.*

About the Author

Patricia Marlett is dedicated to write inspirational novels for both the adult and young reader genres. With a contemporary platform, she pens plots that reflect real life events through drama, intrigue, suspense, humor, and love. Faith-inspiring messages are subtly weaved into each of her themes lending to heartfelt expressions from laughter to tears and always with hope and encouragement.

Patricia always gives honor and glory to God, for her greatest pleasure is writing for the Father. In her latest, *Everlasting Love, God's Greatest Gift* and *Why Prayers Aren't Answered, Understanding Kingdom Principles*, she writes about Him. Visit Patricia at her website, www.patriciamarlett.com, to learn more, view her books, and for contact information.

www.ingramcontent.com/pod-product-compliance
Lightning Source LLC
Chambersburg PA
CBHW061344040426
42444CB00011B/3076